Trump to Harvard:
Go Fund Yourself!
Harvard to Trump:
Let's Make a Deal!

Related Books by Alan Dershowitz

The Preventive State: The Challenge of Preventing Serious Harms While Preserving Essential Liberties

Palestinianism: The Newest Attack on Peace, Human Rights, and Democracy

The Ten Big Anti-Israel Lies: And How to Refute Them with Truth

War Against the Jews: How to End Hamas Barbarism

Defending Israel: The Story of My Relationship with My Most Challenging Client

The Case Against BDS: Why Singling Out Israel for Boycott Is Anti-Semitic and Anti-Peace

The Case Against the Iran Deal

The Case for Moral Clarity: Israel, Hamas and Gaza

The Case Against Israel's Enemies: Exposing Jimmy Carter and Others Who Stand in the Way of Peace

Preemption: A Knife That Cuts Both Ways

The Case for Peace: How the Arab-Israeli Conflict Can Be Resolved

The Case for Israel

Why Terrorism Works: Understanding the Threat, Responding to the Challenge

Chutzpah

Trump to Harvard: *Go Fund Yourself!*
Harvard to Trump: *Let's Make a Deal!*

WHO WILL WIN?

ALAN DERSHOWITZ
PROFESSOR EMERITUS HARVARD LAW SCHOOL

Skyhorse Publishing

Copyright © 2025 by Alan Dershowitz

All Rights Reserved. No part of this book may be reproduced in any manner without the express written consent of the publisher, except in the case of brief excerpts in critical reviews or articles. All inquiries should be addressed to Skyhorse Publishing, 307 West 36th Street, 11th Floor, New York, NY 10018.

Skyhorse Publishing books may be purchased in bulk at special discounts for sales promotion, corporate gifts, fund-raising, or educational purposes. Special editions can also be created to specifications. For details, contact the Special Sales Department, Skyhorse Publishing, 307 West 36th Street, 11th Floor, New York, NY 10018 or info@skyhorsepublishing.com.

Skyhorse® and Skyhorse Publishing® are registered trademarks of Skyhorse Publishing, Inc.®, a Delaware corporation.

Visit our website at www.skyhorsepublishing.com.

Please follow our publisher Tony Lyons on Instagram @tonylyonsisuncertain

10 9 8 7 6 5 4 3 2 1

Library of Congress Cataloging-in-Publication Data is available on file.

Paperback ISBN: 978-1-5107-8580-9
eBook ISBN: 978-1-5107-8581-6

Cover design by Brian Peterson

Printed in the United States of America

Acknowledgments

Thanks to Alan Rothfeld, Jessie Davison, Aaron Voloj, Elon Dershowitz, and Annie Hoyos for their assistance. And to Carolyn Cohen for her love, inspiration, and advice.

Contents

Introduction: The War Between Trump and Harvard ... 1

A. What Does "Meritocracy" Mean? Not Only Grades ... 38

B. What If Khalil Were Pro-Nazi Instead of Pro-Hamas? ... 41

C. Case of Anti-Israel Green Card Holder Seized by ICE Could Be a Close Call for Even the Highest of Courts ... 44

D. Are Trump's Campus Funding Cuts an Attack or Defense of Free Speech? ... 47

E. Cut Federal Funding to Barnard ... 49

F. Harvard Surrenders! University Professor ALAN DERSHOWITZ Reveals the Secret Deal Being Struck with Trump . . . and It'll Make His Woke Colleagues Furious ... 51

G. Need to Disable Iran's Nuclear Weapons Program More Compelling than Ever ... 55

H. Was the *Atlantic*'s Goldberg Wrong in Not Immediately Leaving the Chat? ... 58

I. Gaza: There Are Precedents for Moving People to Secure Peace ... 60

J. Why Have So Many Israelis and Jews Moved to the Right? ... 62

K. Today's Most Pressing Human Rights Violation: Malignant Antisemitism ... 66

L. Israel's Preemptive Attack Is Legally, Morally, and Diplomatically Justified ... 68

Conclusion ... 72

Introduction

The War Between Trump and Harvard

President Donald Trump has declared war against elite American universities, such as Harvard, where I began teaching more than sixty years ago. Trump has threatened to cut off federal funding, end tax exemptions, and limit foreign student visas. Harvard has filed lawsuits and threatened additional legal action. The nation is deeply divided over this conflict. How should Americans who care deeply about universities, about antisemitism, and about the proper role of government respond to this dangerous rift?

From the beginning of this conflict, I have urged a negotiated, compromise resolution (see pages 51–55). It now appears likely that despite bellicose pronouncements from both sides, some compromise my be reached. But that will not end the controversies. It may begin processes of resolution, but fundamental disagreements over policies, principles, actions, and inactions will remain. This book will address these ongoing processes.

As this book goes to press, bombs are dropping and rockets are exploding in Iran and Israel, as the Israeli Defense Forces seek to destroy Iran's nascent nuclear arsenal. Universities are generally out of session during the summer recess, and so the recurring anti-Israel demonstrations have been relocated to the streets, as part of the more general anti-government protests, most recently focusing on immigration policies. But universities will continue to be a central locus of controversy, disagreement, and disruption. And the Trump administration will continue to react—and in the view of many, to overreact—to increasing politicization of educational institutions.

Efforts to defund, deny visas, and take other punitive steps against universities will remain controversial and will generate legal, political, moral, and economic disputes that call for rational discourse. It is the purpose of this volume to contribute to the discourse from the perspective of a public citizen who has been involved in higher education for more than seventy years, sixty-one of which were affiliated with Harvard. I also bring two additional perspectives, having been involved in relevant legal and constitutional challenges, including representing President Trump in his first impeachment trial. Finally, I bring the perspective of a deeply committed Jew and Zionist, though a contrarian one, who has written quite critically over the years of both Judaism and Israel. My special talent, if I have one, is to ask provocative questions rather than provide definitive answers. It is to these questions that I now turn.

There are several basic questions at issue in the decision whether to defund or otherwise punish universities that discriminate against—or apply a double standard to—Jews as victims of discrimination.

The first question is whether it is ever permissible, as a matter of policy and academic freedom, to weaponize governmental funding of universities in an effort to influence their policies.

Another is whether it is constitutional or otherwise legal to cut off governmental funding based on the content of university speech or policies.

Yet another is whether the Trump administration is currently justified in defunding universities such as Harvard and Columbia for their failures to deal effectively with growing antisemitism on their campuses.

And then there is the issue of whether the government can deny student (or faculty) visas to individuals who advocate or promote antisemitism or other actions that violate American policies.

These questions are obviously interrelated and involve overlapping considerations, but they require separate analytical frameworks in order to assure the application of principled decision-making. So let's turn to them individually.

Is it ever permissible, as a matter of principle and academic freedom, for governments to defund or threaten to defund universities in order to influence their policies and actions?

Many faculty members who are strongly opposed to Trump's actions are basing their opposition on general principles that they claim are universally applicable to <u>all</u> economic pressures—but especially those by governments—on <u>any</u> universities that are designed to influence academically related policies. They argue that universities be immune from governmental influences and free to make decisions based on academic considerations.

In order to address that issue in a neutral and principled manner, it is imperative that we go back in history, first to the mid-to-late 1950s, and then to the 1930s and earlier.

In 1954, a unanimous Supreme Court ruled that public schools, including state universities, could not discriminate against African Americans in admission and other policies and actions. Some schools complied. Others resisted. Some students and faculty continued to discriminate. Some harassed Black students. The Ku Klux Klan sent masked and hooded Klansmen to intimidate advocates of desegregation. Some faculty members espoused White supremacy, both inside and outside the classroom. Some university administrators encouraged such racism—others remained silent. Few, if any, actually opposed or tried to prevent it.

Black students may have been equal as a matter of law,

according to the courts, but they were far from equal as a matter of reality on the campuses and in the classrooms. They were victims of de facto discrimination, and most southern universities and political leaders did little or nothing to combat it.

Back in the 1950s southern universities received little or nothing in the way of direct federal funding. There was of course state funding of public universities, as well as federal tax exemptions and benefits. That was the reality back then.

I'm a law professor who for sixty years employed what is called the "hypothetical" or "Socratic" method of teaching about complex legal issues. That method involves constructing hypothetical scenarios that challenged the principles and policies of the students by reframing the "facts" in a way that made them reconsider their initial conclusions.

So let's construct a "hypothetical" based on southern colleges in the 1950s in order to challenge the conclusions reached by liberals, progressives, and even centrists about the current threats to defund and deny tax benefits to Ivy League universities that allegedly apply a discriminatory double standard against Jews, Zionists, and others.

It is clear that the vast majority of academics, students, democrats, and left-leaning individuals today are strongly opposed to the threats and actions of the Trump administration to defund, deny tax benefits, or restrict visas to universities or students. The opposition purports to be based on neutral principles of academic freedom and non-interference by government into the educational processes of universities. Some of these principled opponents—such as former Harvard president Lawrence Summers and Professor Steven Pinker—are actively involved in advocating that their university do more to combat discrimination against Jewish students. Others agree with those who are applying a double standard against Israel and its Jewish supporters. Indeed, some even support those bigots and join in their discriminatory actions. Many opponents believe that the Trump administration doesn't really care about antisemitism and is merely using it as an excuse to take control of universities. Despite their differences, these opponents all claim to share a common principled opposition to governmental intrusion into the educational policies and practices of universities, both private and public.

So now to the testing hypothetical: Would all of these opponents of government intrusion have been equally opposed in principle if the federal government had threatened to cut off funding (if there had been federal funding back then) or deny tax or visa benefits (which did exist) to universities that did not prevent masked KKK students or non-students from harassing Black students and/or blocking their access to class? What if the universities claimed the KKK students had a First Amendment right to march in opposition to Blacks being treated equally? Or if they argued that White faculty members had the academic freedom to advocate White supremacy both inside and outside the classroom? Governor George Wallace and other southern political leaders made these constitutional arguments and praised university administrators who stood up for the constitutional rights of racists. I'm not talking about defending the First Amendment rights of racists to express their views without government censorship. I'm talking about the alleged rights of universities to receive federal financial benefits which they can then use to promote racism.

Where would today's "principled" opponents of any governmental intrusions on academic freedom of universities have stood in my not-so-hypothetical case?

Unless they would have opposed the defunding, loss of tax exemptions, loss of visa restrictions, and other pressures on southern universities that encouraged or tolerated anti-Black racist activities, they cannot claim principled, neutral, and universal opposition to all or any external, governmental financial pressures on universities to change their despicable policies and/or actions.

If they would have supported, or not opposed, financial pressures on southern universities in the 1950s, then their current opposition to the Trump-defunding threats and actions must—if they are not to be hypocritical—be based on non-principled, non-neutral, non-universal factors. These factors could include legal or constitutional objections, or objections limited to the specific Trump threats and actions. Let's turn therefore to the legal, constitutional, and more specific current objections.

Is it unconstitutional or otherwise illegal to cut off governmental funding based on the content of specific policies?
Legal and constitutional objections must also be based on neutral, objective, and universal principles, unless it can be argued that the law accepts a distinction between efforts to protect Black students, as compared to Jewish students. The law accepts no such distinction. Indeed, the Supreme Court held, in a case involving Harvard's admissions policies decided just three years ago, that the law cannot favor Black applicants for admission over Asian, and presumably other, applicants. So any legal objections cannot be based on purported distinctions between Black and Jewish victims of harassment or intimidation.

It can be argued that there are differences among four types of governmental actions that are designed to influence universities: the first being the defunding of <u>future</u> grants to universities; the second being the recission of <u>past</u> grants; the third being the elimination of tax benefits; and the fourth being restrictions on visas to foreign students or faculty.

1. Future Grants

The weakest case would be claims by a university that it was somehow entitled to receive <u>new</u> financial benefits, such as research grants. The government picks and chooses among schools in deciding whether and how much to grant them in the future. No university has the right—constitutional or otherwise—to receive government grants. They may have the right not to be discriminated against on impermissible grounds, such as race, gender, or religion. So if a government decides in its discretion to make research grants for cancer cures, it cannot deny such grants on unconstitutionally impermissible grounds. But the government may surely consider whether potential recipients of its funding comply with the letter and spirit of equal protection laws. Moreover, deference should be given to the grantor in making decisions about future grants, so long as they do not employ legally impermissible criteria.

Accordingly, the constitutional or legal argument against governmental denial of future financial grants is weak, bordering on frivolous. Moreover, if it were applied to the current Trump refusal to make new grants, it would have been equally applicable to my hypothetical case involving future grants to racist schools in the 1950s. I doubt that many objectors to current defunding would have been willing to make constitutional arguments in favor of future funding of such schools.

Universities may have the right, under the First Amendment or principles of academic freedom, to tolerate or even promote racist, antisemitic, or other hate speech, but they have no right to receive federal funding that could be used, directly or indirectly, to encourage such speech.

2. Existing Grants

When it comes to cutting <u>existing</u> grants or the refusal to <u>renew</u> them, the issue will often depend on contractual relationships that govern the grants. Most such contracts give considerable discretion to the grantor regarding termination or continuation. It is possible, however, that some contracts create the kind of reliances that courts traditionally recognize. This is largely a matter of contract law and not of neutral or general principles.

3. Tax Benefits

Tax benefits are governed by laws and regulations as interpreted by the courts. The leading case, involving a conservative Christian university named Bob Jones, permitted the IRS to deny certain exemptions to the school because it discriminated against students based on race and other impermissible grounds. If that precedent is followed by the current Supreme Court, the IRS could eliminate the tax exemptions for schools that apply a double standard against Jewish students in enforcing disciplinary rules regarding harassment, hate speech, and other forms of intimidation. But the president should not influence decisions made by the IRS.

4. Restricting Visas

Withholding visas from foreign students is an untested tactic, but if the denials are based on neutral principles, rather than ethnicity, national origin, race, or religion, they are likely to be upheld.

The hard question would involve denials based on the content of speech or ideology, such as First Amendment advocacy of Intifada or revolution. I believe the courts would uphold such denials if the laws or regulations were carefully drafted. There is no constitutionally protected right of any non-American to enter the country, and the government may impose reasonable conditions and restriction on such entry, even if those conditions could not be lawfully imposed on Americans.

5. Bottom Line

The bottom line is that the Trump administration is likely to prevail in the courts with regard to executive authority over university funding and visas. This is especially so in the absence of congressional pushback or legislative efforts to limit executive powers in these areas. It may lose some cases on procedural grounds involving the denial of due process, but it will generally prevail on the power of the executive branch to defund, to regulate tax benefits, and to deny student and faculty visas.

Despite its bravado in challenging the Trump actions and threats, Harvard and other universities surely understand that they are unlikely to achieve total victory in court, and that even if they win some battles, they are likely to come out behind both in the courts of law and in the court of public opinion. Although most Americans support governmental funding of medical and other pure and applied scientific research, they do not trust universities with mega billion-dollar endowments to allocate the funds they receive away from ideological and political projects and advocacy centers. They are right in such distrust, as evidenced by past and current allocations.

So litigating these issues is not a winning strategy for universities. But neither is appearing to compromise. University presidents and boards cannot be perceived by their hard-left faculty and students to be capitulating to Trump, so they must resist—or appear to resist. The following media headline, therefore, was to be expected: "Harvard 'will not compromise' in lawsuit against Trump administration, [Harvard] president says. (*Jerusalem Post*, April 24, 2025). But the administrations and boards understand that in the end there must be negotiated resolutions both sides can live with and move on. So, at the end of the day, Harvard and other universities <u>will</u> compromise. That is why Harvard deliberately sent mixed messages in response to the administration's tough demands. Publicly, they responded with a belligerent letter vowing to fight, and with statements denying any compromise. This made them heroes among left-wing faculty, students, and media. At the same time, they quietly retained lawyers with close connections to Trump and with reputations as negotiators and compromisers. This sent a not-so-subtle message to downplay the belligerent public posturing and focus on discreet negotiations.

In the end, much of what the Trump administration demanded of Harvard and other universities is justified in law, morality, and academic integrity: meritocratic admissions and hiring and promotions; a single standard for free speech and disciplining of those who violate that standard; more intellectual, ideological, and academic diversity of viewpoints; maintaining the status of the university as a <u>forum</u> for diverse viewpoints, rather than an <u>advocate</u> for certain positions; prohibition against using the classroom, grading, or recommendations to promote personal or political academic preferences; the dismantling of bureaucracies and special programs and departments that promote left-wing ideologies such as DEI, intersectionality, critical race theory, queer theory, Palestinianism, anti-Israelism, anti-imperialism, anti-colonialism, anti-westernism, anti-Christianity, anti-Whitism, anti-Americanism, and other woke and progressive causes; assurances that the universities are not cheating by smuggling these and other biases in low visibility or disguised decision-making.

Some faculty and administrators agree that these changes should be made and that they should have been made years ago by the universities themselves, but they resent the government—especially THIS government—telling them what to do. Others disagree with some or all of these changes on their merits and demerits. While still others believe that the Trump administration doesn't really care about these issues and is just using them as an excuse or justification for imposing its will on Trump-hating universities.

Whatever the actual mix of reasons for opposing these demands, the reality is that the vast majority of faculty members, administrators, and perhaps students want the universities to resist the Trump demands and fight back—even if it results in economic harms.

Nonetheless, the pragmatic needs of universities suggest that negotiations will go forward and agreements will be reached. Reasonable demands should be met, even if they are the result of unreasonable external pressures. Perhaps some type of mediation can be accepted by both sides. The result will almost certainly be agreement about some demands, continued disagreement about others, and postponed decisions about still others. Some forms of funding will be restored; others redirected; still others denied. Both sides will claim victory to their constituencies.

6. What Would a Realistic Compromise Look Like?

No compromise will satisfy all interested parties to this highly visible and contentious dispute between the Trump administration and Harvard University. Even if a compromise satisfied the Harvard administration, it would not satisfy most of the faculty. Nor would it satisfy the other universities. There are, however, some areas of agreement that might be more acceptable than the status quo.

The most important element of any agreement regarding funding is that it achieves its justified goals—especially of ending the current double-standard bias against Jews, Zionists, conservatives and Christians—without endangering medical and other scientific research that depends heavily on federal funding. Defunding should be as precisely targeted as possible against bigoted components within universities, without imposing collateral damage on scientific, medical, or other research that benefits the innocent. Such targeting is not easy to achieve, especially when universities get lump sum and overhead funding that they have the discretion to allocate.

One radical solution would be to end all <u>general</u> university funding and require <u>individual</u> researchers or research groups to apply for specific financing of their projects. This would probably produce some cost ineffectiveness and other practical problems, but it would reduce the likelihood that government funds would be used improperly to support ideological, biased, and otherwise improper projects.

Even purely scientific, medical, and other research can be impacted by ideological considerations. Some such research projects currently employ discriminatory DEI criteria in hiring and promotion. In other words, they do not employ purely meritocratic criteria in their decision-making. To the extent that such DEI criteria compromise with meritocracy, these criteria employ bad science—or, more precisely, they substitute ideological for scientific criteria. Researchers should be entitled to define what constitutes meritocratic criteria for a particular research project. Grades, publications, and other "objective" indicia can be supplemented by more subjective but relevant factors, but race, ethnicity, gender, religion, or sexual preference alone will rarely be relevant to any reasonable definition of meritocracy. If it is claimed to be, then the proponents or practitioners of these non-meritocratic criteria should have the burden of persuasion.

There may be close questions about what constitutes violations of meritocratic principles, and institutional decision-makers, rather than government bureaucrats, should be given discretion in such cases. But there are many cases in which it should be obvious to any reasonable person that the heavy ideological thumb of DEI is overweighted on the scales of meritocracy. Many such cases are so clear that the folksy Justice Potter Stewart's approach is easily applied: as he put it in an unrelated but apt context: "Perhaps I could never succeed intelligibly [in defining hard-core pornography], but I know it when I see it." Any reasonable and objective observer of today's American university knows bias when he sees it. And its presence should be called out and condemned.

If the federal government rejects the extreme approach of defunding all the universities and instead chooses to fund only specific scientific projects, it will not be easy to assure that some money will not end up in the coffers of biased professors or projects. But, by articulating a rule against the funding of such bias, pressures will be placed on university administrators to engage in proper allocations. The result will not be perfect, but it will be better than the status quo where cheating is the rule, not the exception.

The current controversy between the Trump administration and universities that are threatened with defunding is one of extremes—on both sides. The Trump administration is asking <u>too much</u> of universities that legitimately need to preserve academic independence from undue government intrusion. And most universities, led by Harvard, are willing to give <u>too little</u> to assist the government in its legitimate efforts to ensure the equal protection and academic freedom of all students.

The good news is that both sides have room to negotiate and compromise without surrendering their principles. The bad news is that even if negotiated compromises are reached about the specific issue that currently separates the two sides, the problem of pervasive bias and bigotry on campuses will persist—and perhaps even grow worse. This is because bias and bigotry have become cultural, institutional, and inherent in the structure of too many universities. Faculty tenure and bureaucratic inertia will make it difficult, if not impossible, to undo in the short term the damage that has been done to academic neutrality and integrity over the past decades. The obvious bias demonstrated since October 7, 2023, is simply the most recent and visible manifestation of an insidious and dangerous development that has been beneath the surface for years. Now that it is out in the open, there can be efforts to address it. But it will require major institutional changes that will be difficult to achieve, especially in the face of faculty resistance and bureaucratic inertia.

The major cause of the increasing antisemitism, anti-Israelism, and anti-Americanism is the obsessive focus on identity politics—especially race, ethnicity, religion, gender, sexual orientation, and national origin. This focus has been manifested by the creation of identity departments, programs, studies, professorships, funds, scholarships, and other bureaucracies that overemphasize differences based on color, sex, national origin, and other characteristics. At the same time, these different identity groups unite through the concept of "intersectionality"—a phony "academic" construct that seeks to find, or manufacture, artificial common ground among different "marginalized" identity groups. The common thread that both divides and unites is Jews (a religiously based culture based on a combination of theology, nationalism, ethnicity, and history), their state (Israel), and their National Liberation movement (Zionism).

Anything positively Jewish is excluded from intersectionality, because Jews are deemed "privileged." They are among the oppressors of marginalized identity groups, despite the historic reality that Jews, more than any other group, have been on the side of oppressed and marginalized "others." They have been on the forefront of the African American civil rights movement, the various women's movements, civil liberties, LGBTQ marriage and equality, the environment, and other "liberal" and "progressive" causes. Jews and Israelis have been disproportionately supportive of Palestinian rights, including Palestinian statehood. Moreover, Jews have even been victimized by hate crimes more than any group, both in the United States and around the world. Yet they are categorized as privileged oppressors and excluded from intersectionality.

It is true that some universities have Jewish, Holocaust, and even Israel studies departments and programs, but even some of these Jewish "identity" bureaucracies tend to be anti-Zionist, super critical of Jewish organizations, and generally left-wing. Even so, they are generally excluded from intersectionality simply because of their Jewish and/or Israel affiliation and/or funding.

The end result is that Jewish students and faculty who identify with Israel—even if critically—feel isolated on many campuses, especially from faculty, administrators, and departments. They can join Hillel, Chabad, and other Jewish groups, but they get little support from the official university structure. Most faculty members and administrators who privately support Israel refuse to speak out publicly—in striking contrast to the very public opposition to Israel among so many faculty and administrators.

The nasty cousin of "intersectionality" is "diversity, equity, and inclusion." In theory, these positive-sounding goals should be opposed to discrimination, bias, and double standards. As practiced on most campuses, however, the DEI bureaucracy is the major breeding ground for anti-Jewish hate and bigotry. That is because its components are explicitly defined to exclude Jews from its coverage and to include some of the most antisemitic groups.

Consider "diversity." It should clearly include Jews and supporters of Israel, especially now that these groups have become so marginalized and their numbers in the student body so reduced. But "diversity," as defined by the DEI bureaucrats, explicitly excludes Jews, even Jews of color. So does "inclusion." Jews are not included among the categories of identity groups that qualify for "inclusion" under DEI. Indeed, they are sometimes explicitly excluded from inclusion.

"Equity" is perhaps the most discriminatory category. Despite the similarity in its letters, "equity" is the exact opposite of "equality." To paraphrase perhaps the most influential and well-known egalitarian in history, Martin Luther King Jr., equity judges people not by the "content of their character" but rather by the "color of their skin." It treats <u>all</u> black people alike—and deserving of <u>group</u> "equity." And it treats all white people alike—and requiring group sacrifice and "acknowledgment" of "guilt."

Equity is also the precise opposite of meritocracy. Indeed, meritocracy—which judges people on the basis of their <u>individual</u>

accomplishments, merits, and character, rather than their <u>group</u> identity—is the enemy of equity. Individual assessments and evaluations are incompatible with group benefits.

Words and theories aside, in <u>practice</u>, DEI bureaucracies have come to be dominated by Afro-centric, race-focused, progressive radicals. Not surprisingly these bureaucracies have become incubators for knee-jerk anti-Israel policies and activities. Many of the most virulent antisemitic reactions to the Hamas massacres of October 7 were directed, inspired, or sourced from the DEI, ethnic studies, and/or intersectionality bureaucracies. That is not a surmise. It is an easily documented fact. And it has been acknowledged by some universities. Harvard, for example, has changed the name of its DEI office to "The Office of Community and Campus Life." It remains to be seen whether this is merely a cosmetic change or whether there will be a substantive change in the priorities, politics, personnel, and actions of this office.

Dismantling the DEI-intersectionality bureaucracy is a necessary but not sufficient step toward ending the deeply corrosive double standard against Jews and their nation-state. The next essential step—abolishing identity departments and studies programs—will be much harder to achieve. This is because most of the bureaucrats who run the DEI-intersectionality bureaucracies do not have tenure. Many of the professors who teach in the identity departments and programs do have tenure. Their tenure is generally in other, more traditional departments, such as history, political science, or sociology. Since the identity departments and programs themselves do not have any kind of tenure, they could and should be abolished. The propagandists who "teach" in these departments can go back to teaching in their traditional departments. This will not solve the double-standard bias problem, but it will reduce it, because the bigotry will no longer have the imprimatur and resources of a formal department or official program of the university.

In a nutshell, these identity departments and studies programs are not academically neutral in their approach to their subject matter. Their goal is not the search for objective truth. It is advocacy for the identity group they represent. This group may be African Americans, women, gay or transgender people, Palestinians, Native Americans, or any other identity category. It is rare for these departments or programs to be critical of those they purport to study. For example, the misnamed "critical race theory" is rarely critical of the dominant "race theory" espoused by Afro-centric departments or programs. Nor are others that are identity-centric. The striking exception to this general rule is Jewish studies, which is often hypercritical of Israel, Zionism, Jewish organizations, and related issues. Many of these "Jewish" programs, which include Holocaust studies, are desperate to be accepted by the other ethnic, gender, regional, and politicized programs. So to become acceptable, they become super "critical" of anything Israeli. They lean over backward to demonstrate their objectivity toward anything Jewish. The end result is once again a double standard with regard to Israel: The non-Jewish departments tend to be overtly anti-Israel, while the Jewish departments proclaim themselves to be scrupulously "objective" and "self-critical."

In addition to the structural and organizational causes of anti-Israel bias on campuses, there are also social and atmospheric factors that contribute to the widespread and often irrational hatred of the nation-state of the Jewish people. To be "accepted" among one's peers on many campuses today, students—especially, but not exclusively, Jewish students—must demonstrate their universality or lack of support for their own group. This is not demanded of blacks, Muslims, gays, or others within the intersectionality movement. But it has become a litmus test for Jewish students and faculty who seek acceptability among their dominantly left-wing peers. The only options for these wannabes is: a) joining the anti-Israel mob; b) silence; or c) lack of acceptance. There is no fourth option: One cannot openly support Israel, even while disagreeing with many of its policies and actions, and become acceptable among civil rights, environmental, LGBTQ, Native American, and other "progressive" or even "liberal" advocacy groups. The Berkeley law school situation demonstrates that reality: Numerous identity groups enacted mandatory prohibitions against Zionists speaking to their members. Jews who wanted to speak would, presumably, have to renounce any support for Israel's right to exist as a condition of being allowed to speak on any subject. So the Dean of the law school—Erwin Chemerinsky, a believer in Israel's right to exist, a critic of current Israeli policies, and an expert on constitutional law—would be prohibited from criticizing the overruling of *Roe v. Wade* in front of a women's law group!

The chilling impact—both overt and covert—on political expression is incalculable but real. And this at a public law school whose censorial clubs receive financial support from the government.

So the increase of bigotry against all things Jewish will not be reversed by reports or other remedies now under consideration. The current hatred runs too deep in the consciousness and unconsciousness of too many students and faculty. They refuse to recognize their own bigotry and ignorance. They honestly (sometimes dishonestly) think they are right, much like many southern bigots who hated Blacks, and many German students who hated Jews, thought they were right.

It will take generational changes in the hearts and souls of those who influence university life to completely undo the pervasive and irrational double standard that affects so much of today's campus life. But the process must begin somewhere, and structural institutional changes are an essential first step.

Recently Harvard published a report acknowledging multiple

failures—structural, academic, atmospheric, personnel—in stemming antisemitism, anti-Israelism, and other manifestations of double-standard bigotry. The report was released at this time as a response to the threat of defunding by the Trump administration. Even so, the Harvard administration, in order to throw a bone to its radical faculty and students, simultaneously issued a report purporting to show anti-Muslim, anti-Arab, and anti-Palestinian activities on campus. This is a transparent effort to suggest a false "moral equivalence" between the massive and pervasive anti-Jewish activities on the one hand and the minimal and general reactive "Islamophobia" on the other. Anyone with eyes, ears, and a conscience will see this ploy for what it is: yet another manifestation of the malignant double standard.

The report on antisemitism—despite its effort to be evenhanded, moderate, and careful—documented numerous instances of Jewish and Israeli hatred not only by students, but by faculty and administrators as well. The resemblance to what occurred in German universities in the 1930s should not be understated: In both contexts, Jewish students were harassed, silenced, demeaned, isolated, and treated as second class and worse. Obviously matters became much worse by the early 1940s, but the parallels to the treatment of Jews in the mid-1930s are striking.

The School of Public Health and the Divinity School were the worst offenders in the systematic effort to marginalize, delegitimize, cancel, and silence Jews who refused to denounce Israel, Zionism, and sometimes even their religious heritage. Being a Jewish supporter of Israel—even a critical one—was not so different in these Harvard schools from being a Jewish student at the university of Heidelberg in 1935.

David Wolpe, a moderate Zionist who is often quite critical of Israel, recounted his year at the Harvard Divinity School in an article about the academic year (2023–24) he spent there as a visiting scholar and teacher. He titled his article "Harvard is spraying perfume on a sewer." He described "the sewer" as follows:

> Students were insulted, shunned, harassed and hounded in a hundred ways. An Israeli student was mobbed and assaulted at a "die-in" protest days after October 7. "Privilege trainings" for Jewish students were run by the university. Another student, a former soldier in the Israel Defense Forces, told me she was afraid to walk alone to her dorm room. Students were ghosted by longtime friends for expressing sympathy with Israel. One was told by friends it would hurt their careers to "associate with a Zionist." Professors, in courses on Israel, removed all Israeli sources from the syllabus. Required reading in a Public Health course titled Settler Colonial Determinants of Health teaches that "Zionism manipulated Judaism as a religion to reinterpret history and redefine Jewishness in terms of ethnic belonging."
>
> So as anxious students flocked to my office, I was shocked but not surprised to see the hostility continue unabated. There was memorably a cartoon posted by a Harvard faculty group on Instagram showing a Jewish hand hanging an Egyptian and a black man—a retread of a cartoon from the 1960s that was condemned at the time by black leaders as antisemitic. This cartoon was, to quote the report, "circulated by groups of pro-Palestinian Harvard students, staff, and faculty on social media." *Faculty!* That is Harvard in 2024.

Wolpe saw constant comparisons between the genocidal murder of six million Jews and Israel's legitimate defense against efforts to destroy it and murder its residents:

This false moral equivalency is everywhere at Harvard and places like it. And it was present [with the publication of the Harvard reports.] The antisemitism report was published concurrently with a report on Islamophobia. (It is worth noting that according to the FBI's 2023 Hate Crime statistics, 68 percent of all religion-based hate crimes were committed against Jews, and 8.7 percent against Muslims.)

Any American of any religious stripe or political denomination should condemn any bigotry toward another group. Full stop. And I don't doubt that Muslim students felt uneasy or even rhetorically attacked. But the idea that the venom directed against the two groups was in any way equal, or equally motivated, is absurd.

For example, the Muslim students in the Presidential Task Force on Combating Anti-Muslim, Anti-Arab, and Anti-Palestinian Bias report complained of the perils of wearing a keffiyah. ("I was harassed when I wore a keffiyeh at my . . . work-study job"). I do not doubt that this occurred—and perhaps on many occasions. In my observation however, the keffiyah was the fashion accessory of the season, whether you hailed from Riyadh, Saudi Arabia or Greenwich, Connecticut. You could not walk across campus without seeing scores of students and some faculty in a keffiyah, among the far, far fewer kippot and Jewish stars. At one point, the statue of John Harvard was draped in a keffiyah; I never saw him wrapped in tefillin.

There was also a striking asymmetry of action: Zionist students did not camp out in Harvard Yard; They did not break into classrooms; They did not come with bullhorns (as I myself witnessed) into local restaurants and chant in Arabic, "From the river to the sea, Palestine will be Arab." Their teaching assistants did not offer passes on exams to attend rallies, or attend rallies with them. They did not insist on wearing masks outdoors, so they could yell slogans with impunity. They did not continually yell slogans in the yard after they were understood to be eliminationist. . . .

These two reports should not have been issued in tandem; it is an example of "bothsidesism" on steroids.

This is Wolpe's conclusion:

But what the report offers no solution for is that there is a deep ideological commitment among much of the faculty—particularly in the humanities and social sciences—that is anti-Western, anti-Israel, and often antisemitic. The Islamophobia report mentions "donors" (read: Jewish donors) who influence policy, but the antisemitism report does not focus on millions flowing from places like Qatar. The confluence of Islamism, old-line Christian antisemitism, and hard progressive antagonism to the Western and Israel project produced a perfect storm in places like Harvard Divinity School. Without a vast unlearning—among the *faculty*, not just the students—all the reports in the world will not change the atmosphere on campus. We will only be spraying perfume on a sewer.

The antisemitism report concluded with the recommendation that Harvard leaders should combat "with <u>equal</u> resolve" anti-Muslim, Arab, and Palestinian "bias." This would be like southern schools in the 1950s being asked to combat with equal resolve anti-white and anti-black bias. Harvard's negative bias is one sided: against Jews and their nation-state. Harvard's positive bias has been equally one-sided in favor of only one group—Palestinians. This focus on negative anti-Israelism and positive pro-Palestinianism cannot be countered by "equal resolve." Harvard must directly confront its malignant one-sided bias by un-equal resolve to end its double-standard bigotry against Jews and Israel.

The report itself repeatedly documents this bigoted double standard but then essentially ignores it in its proposals. Here are some striking examples from the report's description of events at the Divinity School and the Chan School of Public Health:

One student described the experience at the Divinity School as follows:

> Two years before October 7th, I enrolled in a course at the Harvard Divinity School. Its title was Religion and Peace in Israel/Palestine, and its introduction read: "In this course, we will explore the Israeli/Palestinian conflict, with particular focus on identifying and analyzing the varied and complex roles of religions and promoting both violence and peace. This will be examined through engagement with Israeli and Palestinian literature. . ."
>
> The lecturer began the class with what she called a moment of candor: "The discourse is saturated with the Israeli narrative," she explained to the students, most of whom were Christians from American communities encountering academic material on the conflict for the first time. "Therefore, I decided, with a heavy heart, to remove Israeli sources from the syllabus. We will focus solely on Palestinian literature because power disparities, methodology, and conscience demand it."
>
> The measured manner in which this was delivered made me suspect it was a planned drama, but it took time to grasp its significance. . . .
>
> As we progressed in the lessons, my classmates' antipathy toward me, the sole Israeli in the course, intensified.

And who could blame them? Based on the course material, it was hard not to conclude that Zionism is a project of fictive and mobilized religiosity, while Palestinian identity is authentic and rooted. My attempts to highlight Zionism's story as a movement of liberal pragmatism—which sought to break free from what was perceived as the oppressive shackles of Jewish law and religion in the diaspora—were of little help. Nor did recounting the story of the Jewish community and the pre-Zionist land of Israel, the aliyah of the disciples of the Vilna Gaon, or the history of Safed.

In one of the lessons, a tearful Presbyterian seminary student proclaimed, "Israel was built on cruel religious manipulation. If only we had been able to channel this understanding into American activism we would have reaped the benefits."

The day after October 7th, more than 30 student organizations published a letter declaring Israel solely and entirely responsible for Hamas violence against it. Recently, during a joint lecture hosted by the law and divinity schools, a proposal was even raised that the United States should arm Gaza against Israel. Many members of those organizations had sat with me in that theology course.

Another student described the Chan School:

Chan has a truth; this is just how we think; Chan has never had a single event that is pro-Israel or even neutral, it is all very one sided. [Harvard Chan School student]

Weekly [at the Chan School] there were [events hosted by the Palestinian Program of FXB]—there were a ton of flyers around the school, a seeming constant presence to students that

> *"the most important thing in public health is Palestine"* and there is only one acceptable view. *[Harvard Chan School student]*

The report continues:

> Notably, every Jewish and non-Jewish student who raised concerns about the Palestinian Program with the Task Force also expressed either personal ambivalence or even opposition to the ongoing Israeli military operations in Gaza, as well as deep concern about the health and well-being of Palestinians. At the same time these students felt there was no place for them in such programs at the Harvard Chan School unless they adopted a pervasive yet at best incomplete framing of facts and history that had become, in their view, almost universal in the School.

The task force also received numerous complaints about the Chan School's course on the "Settler Colonial Determinants of Health," which was taught by a leader of the Palestinian Program.

> Many objected to political litmus tests. One notable example involved the "Settler Colonial Determinants of Health" course, taught annually at the Harvard T.H. Chan School of Public Health. A 2021 email . . . distributed to the full department, described the course as part of a broader initiative that ultimately resulted in the creation of two courses:
>> The Department has developed a course on *Decolonizing Global Health* . . . and a course offered this Winter session, *The Settler Colonial Determinants of Health*. . . ; The Brown Bag Seminar has diversified its speakers.

The first instructor of the first class mentioned in this email "Decolonizing Global Health," described their vision for the topic on social media in a post that students shared with us:

> ~"Decolonizing global health"~ means standing against actual material (settler) colonialism, not talking about DEI in academia. It means standing up for a free Palestine.

The report "found this activism negatively affecting the academic mission of Harvard."

Some across academia, including at Harvard, have been engaged in a broad effort to show (as an article recently assigned to students in an elective course at one School said) that the relationship between modern Jews and any origin story in the territory of the British Mandate of Palestine is ahistorical. A cluster of academics elsewhere promote this theory, disputing any link between the Jewish population in the ancient Middle East, Jews in the modern Western world, and the Land of Israel (as it is known in the Jewish tradition). This polemical literature is contradicted by scholarship demonstrating longstanding connections between ancient Middle Eastern and modern Jewish populations as well as the religious concepts, charitable networks, and migration flows that have long connected Jews to the land of Israel, <u>distinct</u> though those bonds may be from <u>modern</u> Zionism. However, some have succeeded in turning this subject into an academic debate, and faculty assigning these materials may do so without also assigning readings that offer differing perspectives.

This rhetoric can be, moreover, particularly harmful when applied to Israeli students at Harvard, whose own views about the political situation in Israel/Palestine, we should know, vary widely.

A deeply troubling application of this strategy we have heard about across Harvard is an attempt by student activists to <u>drive Israeli</u> students (and Jewish students who feel connected to Israel) out of <u>student life</u>. This often takes the form of "shunning." Israeli Jewish students complained to our task force of great difficulties participating in student organizational and club life, for example, and told us alarming stories of people walking away from them mid-conversation as soon as it came up that they were from, for instance, Tel Aviv. As American Jews at Harvard often have Israeli immigrant heritage or other connections to Israel, this type of organizing often undermines the ability of Jewish students to participate in Harvard's learning environment.

Faculty in some parts of Harvard also expressed fear that their colleagues would not vote to appoint a Zionist or an Israeli to a faculty position in their departments.

Nor is this anti-Israel bigotry limited to the Divinity and Chan schools. Although they are the worst, they are not alone. Anti-Jewish bigotry has been pervasive both within and outside of Harvard for several years:

This new era of pro-Palestine organizing has brought new tactics to the table. One tactic focuses on identifying and leveraging organizations and structures that were susceptible to pro-Palestinian messaging and could be mobilized against Israel. Initially, scholarly associations were a common target of this tactic. For example, around 2010 a group of anti-Israel academics worked to take control of the board of the American Studies Association with the apparent goal of (among other things) issuing a statement supporting the boycott of Israeli universities. At Harvard, such tactics were echoed by activists in the local graduate student labor union who, after October 7th, issued their own statement condemning Israel, prompting the resignation of many Jewish members and their allies. Similarly, as we will describe in Chapter 4, some Harvard <u>instructors</u> appear in recent years to have used courses and academic programs at certain Harvard Schools as focal points for a particular type of pro-Palestine politics and activism.

A second tactic that some pro-Palestinian organizers have adopted is trying to inject discussion of the Palestinian cause wherever possible and to use disruptive tactics to raise awareness of the cause. At Harvard, student life cycle events that are meant to build a common civic identity as Harvard students (such as First-Year Convocation at Harvard College, and residency "Match Day" at Harvard Medical School) have become sites of pro-Palestinian protests as protestors seek to inject "the question of Palestine" into areas of student life. At a student-led conference in 2024, pro-Palestinian students at one School ensured that Palestine was a major topic, and the pro-Palestinian "virtual tote bag" given to participants contained an "action toolkit." (This School's leadership responded admirably to this event, acting promptly and decisively to remove the irrelevant material and re-focusing the event on its intended purpose.) Some faculty at Harvard and elsewhere have sought to support and inspire students to engage in these types of protests by excusing them from class, by signaling support with symbolic clothing, or by saying so directly or indirectly. We found evidence that certain faculty were injecting highly partisan discussions of the Israeli-Palestinian conflict and of American Jewish groups in courses that had no direct connection with these subjects, apparently even before October 7th.

Part—but only part—of the reason for Harvard's anti-Jewish and anti-Israel turn is the dramatic—too soft a word—decrease in the number of Jewish students at Harvard. When Harvard's anti-Jewish quotas began to weaken following World War II, the percentage of Jewish students at the college reached "between 20–25%." Now it is "much smaller," below the 10% anti-Jewish quota established by President A. Lawrence Lowell half a century earlier. The report attributes this decline to "changes in admission practices that sought greater racial and ethnic diversity" (p.32) as well as "how [applicants] sold themselves to Harvard in the application process" (p.13).

This later statement strongly implies that applicants received an advantage for emphasizing their one-sided solidarity with Palestine. This implication was corroborated by the report's recommendation that "Harvard should change [its] admission policy to reflect what campus should look like: people listening to each other."

Other examples in the report are as follows:

> Jewish students told us stories of Harvard-run "<u>privilege trainings</u>" where they were told that they were deemed to be privileged by not only by dint of being identified as White but also because of their Jewishness, which allegedly endowed them with an even higher level of privilege. This discourse creates absurd situations in which Jewish students from working class backgrounds are told by authority figures that they are oppressing classmates from much wealthier backgrounds and with stronger preparation for academic and social life at Harvard. These sorts

of exercises are deeply poisonous and risk creating barriers between students who often naturally seek to connect through common interests.

We also encountered an effort by some to redefine antisemitism in a way that drains the term of meaning. For example, while we were writing this report a prominent Jewish leader on campus made public statements about what this person saw as antisemitism in a University program. We then received complaints from Jewish and non-Jewish Harvard affiliates that essentially inverted the accusation, claiming that the prominent Jewish leader was antisemitic and that the program the individual had criticized was the only unit on campus in their view fighting antisemitism. This position changes antisemitism from a serious bias worth combating into an accusation that is strategically deployed in order to obfuscate legitimate concerns. Similarly, 500 Harvard affiliates wrote a letter in Fall 2024 condemning an outside Jewish organization's scheduled antisemitism training session at Harvard. Such a pre-emptive response towards anti-bias education would be hard to imagine if the topic were biased against any other group.

The report found that:

Substantial numbers of Jewish students feel that since October 7th they have lived in an increasingly hostile atmosphere in their residences, classes, organizations, and clubs, as well as in the public spaces of Harvard Yard and the Science Center Plaza.
- Many Israeli students have felt particularly victimized, often in the form of social shunning.

- Fear of encountering hostility has led some Jewish students to conceal their Jewish identity from classmates.

The report noted the widespread perceptions of a double standard:

- There were widespread perceptions that anti-Israeli and anti-Jewish expression are tolerated in a way that hostile rhetoric towards other groups would not be; that some of Harvard's offices for Equity, Diversity, Inclusion and Belonging have not taken antisemitism seriously; and that discipline against students who engaged in bullying, harassment, and intimidation has been lax.

The report describes an account of an email received by students:

> The Task Force received a report that a Teaching Fellow at Harvard Law School sent an email to students in their class on October 10, 2023, which included the following:
>> I have tried to normalize the practice of bringing your whole identities and ideologies to the law school and classroom. I am sure you have been apprised of the ongoing violence in Gaza. To say the least, the news may seem overwhelming and confusing. I remain a resource for you all as a peer and TF to help process what we are seeing. I found that spaces like the event below, a vigil at 7pm tonight at the Harvard Science Center, are very grounding. I invite you to take time to process your emotions, develop your commitments, and be in the community.
>
> The student described in a letter to the Task Force how this made them feel:

> [The Teaching Fellow] made no mention of the horrific terrorist attacks on civilians in Israel and made it seem that this was a one-sided issue, echoing the abhorrent statement written by the Harvard Palestinian Society Committee that was released days earlier and signed by 34 student organizations. . . .

These experiences appear to be widespread, with reports emerging from students in Harvard College, Harvard Law School, Harvard Graduate School of Education, Harvard Divinity School, Harvard T.H. Chan School of Public Health, Harvard Kenneth C. Griffin Graduate School of Arts and Sciences, and Harvard Medical School. Israeli students, both Jewish and non-Jewish, encountered a more severe version of the same problem since their Israeli identity is often very obvious to their fellow Harvard community members:

> On paper, I went to the best . . . school in the world, but Jewish students weren't really part of the vision they had for their diverse community. I largely felt that there was a problem but nobody wanted to do anything about it. It just seemed to be the case that antisemitism was just okay. And as an Israeli it was just okay to alienate me and not include me. Friends of mine were bullied for being friends with me—one was told that it would "hurt his career to associate with a Zionist and to be publicly associated with a Zionist." He posted a picture of us studying together on Instagram and people attacked him for being with me. I never even did pro-Israel things—I just existed [as an Israeli and a Jew]. This ruined my experience. I was cheated out of what I should get to experience as a student at Harvard. Going to Harvard meant everything to me—to spend [my time at Harvard] being bullied and ostracized was horrible. I was not invited to participate in

> *the social life of my [cohort] because of this and I missed out on opportunities. [Graduate Student]*
>
> The experiences students related, such as overhearing friends urging classmates to drop a student solely because of that student's Jewish and Israeli identity, are deeply concerning. One faculty member told the Task Force that students had expressed interest in their course but ultimately decided not to enroll because the faculty member was "a Zionist." Similarly, a student reported to us overhearing a non-Jewish classmate ask another student about a Jewish peer: "Is she a fanatical racist Zionist or just a Jew?"
>
> Some HMS faculty, staff, and students characterized the dominant political atmosphere at HMS as a monoculture. Unfortunately, we were told, Jews do not do well in this narrative, where "Jews are the oppressors and [part of being good and supporting health means] stopping colonialism and Israel." In recent years, HMS has embraced an expansive view of the role of health professionals in promoting public health, for example by training its new students how to become advocates and activists on issues related to public health and encouraging them to leverage their roles as physicians to affect social change along multiple dimensions. Importantly, while this political framework suggests a worthy concern about certain forms of discrimination, many community members expressed concern that this focus seems limited to groups "underrepresented in medicine" or those experiencing "adverse health outcomes." These categories, they noted, do not include Jews or Israelis.

The report attributes some of this to the growing influence of junior faculty, which doesn't bode well for the future. One faculty member expressed concern to the task force that:

> The general shift of power from regular faculty and to para-academic administrators has played an outsized role in the politicization and radicalization of academia and its intellectual and reputational decline. In the case at hand, it is hard to believe that years of one-sided programming by such appointees has not played a role in "hatred of the Jewish state" [becoming] the default position across campus.

While this perspective reflects the view of one faculty member, the Task Force acknowledges the potential influence of such a power shift on campus climate. In this regard, we heard from students expressing concerns about prejudiced behavior among some teaching fellows and junior personnel. Additionally, the Task Force has received reports alleging that some senior faculty members espouse anti-Israeli biases and expressed suspicion toward the Jewish community, suggesting their potential influence in shaping campus climate should not be disregarded.

At several Harvard schools—particularly the public health, divinity, and education schools—there were programs that expressly or implicitly stated their goal as the "training of pro-Palestinian activists" (p.8). This translates into the training of <u>anti-Israel</u> activists, which in turn translates into the training of anti-Jewish activists. Those kinds of biased advocacy programs have no legitimate role in a university. They surely should not be funded by taxpayers.

The bottom line of the report is that there is qualitatively far more antisemitism at Harvard than there was during its "golden age" ("from the 1960s until the 2010s"). The sad reality appears to be that African American and LGBTQ students, faculty, and administrators are among the most antisemitic. The increase in antisemitism and anti-Israelism corresponds to the "changes in

American demographics and Harvard's admission policies"; away from meritocracy and toward identity-based admission preferences; away from Jews and toward groups with higher levels of opposition to Israel.

> The changing composition of student bodies may also partially explain the growing polarization on campus around the Israeli-Palestinian conflict. Over the past thirty years, colleges throughout the United States have diversified their student bodies, partly to reflect demographic changes in the country, and in part to redress past discrimination against underrepresented minorities. Students of Middle Eastern, South Asian, and African heritage have been in the forefront of support for the Palestinian cause nationwide.

The former Harvard admissions dean, Wilburt Bender, warned that "if admissions were based on intelligence alone, there would be too many Jews at Harvard." (p.37) Now that admissions are based heavily on identity rather than merit alone, the number of Jewish admittees has fallen dramatically. This has contributed to the polarization on campus.

As an Arab-Israeli student said:
> Instead of <u>diversity moderating</u> people, people become more extreme. One Palestinian student showed up [at Harvard], talking with Israelis. By the end [of their time at Harvard, the student] cut off ties with Israelis and posted [on social media] in favor of Hamas.

The report heard similar statements from many other people, including faculty and staff who work closely with students:

> They saw Harvard as a place where, over time, many

students' politics become more radical and where students become less tolerant of people who disagree with them. Faculty who work closely with students told us that in this generation, students too often feel they are carrying the weight of their identities, since they say that is how they sold themselves to Harvard in the application process. This positioning contributes to a kind of effective polarization that, we believe, Harvard has neither anticipated nor developed a set of tools to counteract. Reversing this polarization will require hard decisions and strong leadership. The Israeli Arab student we spoke with provided a suggestion that we think is crucial for moving forward:

> Harvard should change [its] admissions policy to reflect what campus should look like: people listening to each other.

The report expressed "frustration" with what it found:

> Moreover, if a faculty member teaching a course unrelated to Israel/Palestine incorporates derogatory references to "Israelis" and "Zionists," as we were told happened at multiple Harvard Schools over the course of the 2023–24 academic year, the University is likely to respond with some frustration, even exasperation, but may, nonetheless, strive to defend the academic freedom of its instructors.

The proposals offered by the report may improve the situation at the extremes. It does more, perhaps, than merely spray perfume on the sewer. But it fails to propose the kind of institutional and cultural reforms that are necessary to treat the malignancies that threaten to kill Harvard and other universities. Among the reforms necessary to address the root cause of double-standard bigotry are the following:

1. A return to meritocratic admissions, hiring, and promotion policies.
2. A return to rigorous, meritocratic, blind grading—as a check on meritocratic admissions and as a criterion for judging success of teaching and student performance.
3. The end of the non-meritocratic diversity, equity, and inclusion (DEI) regimes and bureaucracies.
4. The end of ethnic, gender, regional, religious, sexual preference, and other identity-based departments, studies, programs, and other advocacy centers that have become incubators for anti-Jewish bigotry.
5. A reduction in "globalization" and the prioritization of a more domestic focus.
6. A deliberate effort to create a more intellectually, ideologically, politically, and economically diverse student, faculty and bureaucratic community.
7. The application of a single standard of free speech, academic freedom, and discipline.
8. The creation of, and support for, a cultural environment in which every member of the community is judged on the basis on the content of their character, their efforts and achievements, as well as other meritocratic individual criteria, rather than group identification.
9. The creation of governance mechanisms and criteria that foster the above values.

Even the achievement of all of these goals will not guarantee the end of the current entirely unacceptable situation that plagues and threatens to destroy so many institutions of higher education. But without these changes—every single one of them—the future is bleak and is heading in the wrong direction. An old joke defines a pessimist as one who believes that things are so bad they can't get worse; and an optimist as one who quickly responds, "Yes, they can!" The bigotries and double standards that currently afflict so many elite universities are indeed "so bad," but they can and will get worse—unless the trajectory is dramatically altered.

There will be massive resistance to change by radical faculty, students, administrators, and alumni who believe that the current trajectory is in the right—in this case the left—direction. It will take both internal and external pressures, including but not limited to governmental and private donors, to bring about needed change. It would be best, of course, if the changes came entirely from within, but institutional constraints such as tenure and bureaucratic inertia make that unlikely. The future of our universities is too important to permit the inmates alone to continue to run the campuses. They had their chances, and they have failed. Now it is time—indeed it is long overdue—for academic institutions to be restored to their appropriate mission: namely, objective and neutral teaching, learning, and research. The challenge is to construct governance structures for universities that can implement these goals without undue governmental or ideological influence. A difficult but essential task!

A. What Does "Meritocracy" Mean? Not Only Grades

Most Americans believe in meritocracy as described by Martin Luther King Jr.'s dream of a day when all people are judged not "by the color of their skin but by the content of their character." But the concept of meritocracy does not have a singular meaning. Nor does the "content of their character" mean the same thing to different people.

Meritocracy has several possible meanings. It can mean <u>current performance evaluation</u>, without regard to the past or future. Pilots, surgeons, athletes, stock pickers, and others in similar positions are generally judged by their current ability to do the job best. We do not really care whether our surgeon commendably overcame hardships to become a good surgeon. If there is a "better" surgeon—with a higher rate of success and a lower rate of failures—who overcame no hardships, a rational patient would select him or her. So would a rational airplane owner choosing a pilot, a rational investor selecting a stock picker, a rational orchestra leader deciding on a first violinist, or a rational coach drafting a power forward or fast ball pitcher. These are <u>empirical</u> not <u>moral</u> decisions. Perhaps, in an extreme case, a decision-maker might bypass the empirically <u>best</u> candidate because that candidate was so morally compromised that the decision-maker is willing to sacrifice the best outcome on the altar of a higher morality. That is a choice only some would make about some outcomes. This first definition of meritocracy looks only at the present and the immediate future.

The second definition takes a longer view of the future. It looks at each <u>candidate's likely trajectory</u>. How far into the future one looks depends on the task at hand. Selecting applicants for admissions to college, professional or graduate school requires a prediction of success over a relatively short period of time (four or so years). For faculty members, pilots, orchestra members a bit longer. But these judgments are also primarily empirical, not moral.

The third definition is largely moral. It requires an assessment of <u>deservingness that goes back to the past</u>, sometimes the distant past. The candidate is judged not only based on his/her current or future performance level, but also on the distance they have traveled and the barriers they have had to overcome to get where they now are. A Black applicant from a dysfunctional family or a White candidate from Appalachian family affected by fentanyl would get an advantage over an equally, or even more, qualified person. This could have an empirical component if the decision-maker reasonably concludes that overcoming <u>past</u> disadvantages is relevant to predicting <u>future</u> success. But the <u>moral</u> component obviously plays an important, often decisive, role in rewarding past indicia of "character" without regard to the future trajectory.

In theory, these three descriptions of meritocracy differ, but in practice they may overlap in particular situations, especially when it comes to race as a factor in decision-making. But race <u>alone</u> should <u>never</u> be a factor in <u>any</u> decision based on <u>any</u> definition of meritocracy, since race <u>alone</u> is <u>always</u> entirely irrelevant. A wealthy Black applicant whose mother is a federal judge, whose father owns a hedge fund and who attended elite private schools should never be given any advantage over a more qualified White applicant from a poor family. If the Black applicant experienced discrimination on account of his or her race, that experience may count for something—not much—but the same would be true for a privileged Asian or Jewish student who experienced discrimination.

A fourth possible category of moral preference includes group reparations for collective past discrimination. But that does not fit into any reasonable definition of meritocracy—a concept that requires <u>individual</u> rather than <u>group</u> evaluation. Judging someone on the basis of group affiliation is judging them on the basis of race—in clear violation of King's dream. It rewards underserving individuals based on accidental group affiliation.

Institutions should be given discretion in defining meritocracy, but once they decide on, and make public, their definition and criteria, they shouldn't be allowed to cheat, fudge, or lie about what they are doing. That is exactly what universities are doing today. They are cheating because their objective is not to achieve any kind of meritocracy. Nor is it to achieve diversity. They have only one goal, but they cannot acknowledge it. Their only goal is to fill a quota of Black students between 13 and 17 percent—regardless of other considerations. That goal is, of course, illegal, unconstitutional, and immoral. So they must disguise it.

Other institutions have different goals. NBA teams, which are dominantly Black, do not care about diversity or moral meritocracy. They draft and trade players solely on the basis of current and short-term performance qualifications: They want to win this season and next. I pick doctors solely on the basis on current skills: I want this operation to go well. Good music directors select performers from behind a screen in order to protect against unconscious bias: They want to hear, not see the musicians.

So let us have an honest discussion of what "meritocracy" should and does mean. That has been sorely lacking since Martin Luther King Jr. dreamt his dream of equality.

B. What If Khalil Were Pro-Nazi Instead of Pro-Hamas?

What if a German neo-Nazi who supported the Holocaust had received a visa and green card and then proceeded to lead pro-Nazi encampments and protests against Blacks, gays, and Jews?

Question: If the government moved to revoke his status and deport him, would there be academic and left-wing protests against the alleged violation of his First Amendment rights? To help us answer that question, let's go back nearly half a century in time. In 1977 a group of neo-Nazis were denied the right to march through a neighborhood of Jewish Holocaust survivors in Skokie, Illinois. The American Civil Liberties Union—on whose national board I then served—made the courageous decision to defend their right on First Amendment grounds. This led to massive resignations from the organization and a significant cutback in contributions. I agreed with the decision then and continue to do so.

Now, nearly fifty years later, the ACLU has decided to defend the right of Mahmoud Khalil not to be deported for leading disruptive encampments and leafletting protests on the Columbia University campus. A senior ACLU attorney put it this way:

> This seems like one of the biggest threats, if not the biggest threat to First Amendment freedoms in 50 years. It's a direct attempt to punish speech because of the viewpoint it espouses.

I am aware of no resignations or protests against this ACLU decision. To the contrary, Khalil has become something of a hero: Thousands of students, faculty and others have signed petitions supporting him. There are demonstrations in support of him and his views at Harvard and on other campuses.

There are of course differences, but they cut against Khalil, who is not a citizen, whereas the nasty Nazis were. Khalil has a visa and green card, but they may have been obtained fraudulently. If Khalil had truthfully answered the visa application question whether he intends to provide "support to terrorist organizations," his applications would have been denied. If he answered it falsely, as he presumably did, he would have obtained his documents by fraud. In that case it should be revoked, and he should be deported.

Unlike the Nazis for whom there were no rallies and who were universally condemned by those who defended their free speech rights, many of those who are defending Khalil's free speech rights are also supporting the substance of what he has said and done. As one of the speakers at the Harvard rally acknowledged: "It is important that we understand that we are not simply here in defense of free speech or constitutional rights. Our fight cannot end nor begin at the restriction of free speech." He insisted that protestors should recognize that Khalil was arrested because he specifically advocated for pro-Palestine causes. They claim that his deportation is in retaliation for his opposition to Israel, describing him as a humanitarian and human rights activist. This despite evidence that Khalil expressed support for Hamas following its barbarism of October 7 and probably before. Others are remaining silent about the content of his despicable views, refusing to condemn them as they did the Nazis.

The question is: Why the difference?

To me, the Khalil case bears a striking resemblance to Skokie, because what Khalil has supported bears a striking resemblance to what the Nazis advocated. In fact, his First Amendment claims are weaker because he is not a citizen.

Imagine if the Trump administration were seeking to deport a green-card holding leader of the Ku Klux Klan who had led masked demonstrations that glorified the lynching of Blacks, the raping of women, and the beheading of babies. I doubt that the current ACLU would be defending his free speech rights. But even if they did, I'm certain there would be mass resignations by members. There would be few if any petitions or demonstrations on behalf of the KKK green-card holder, and no one except fellow racists would be making him a hero.

So why the difference? Khalil claims a First Amendment right to demonize Israel and to glorify the Al-Aqsa Storm, which is the name Hamas had given the barbaric events of October 7. Likewise, the Nazis claimed the right to march through Skokie, glorifying the Holocaust and demonizing its survivors. The difference is not in the First Amendment, under which the Nazi claims are stronger. It is in the way in which too many students, civil libertarians, and the media are treating Khalil now, as contrasted with the way the Nazis were treated back then.

The First Amendment is designed to protect the most despicable hate speech, so long as it does not constitute incitement to immediate violence. That is why both the Nazis and Khalil should be treated similarly by the courts of law, without regard to the content of their speech. But the court of public opinion should also treat them similarly, as it has not done. Both the KKK and Hamas advocate violence against vulnerable minorities. It is constitutionally justifiable to support such advocacy of violence through speech and demonstrations (though not through material support of designated terrorist groups, an issue not directly involved in these cases.) But it is not morally justifiable to defend the substance of what Khalil has supported, any more than it would be to defend the substance of the views of the despicable Nazis who marched in Skokie.

Even with regard to the free speech and academic freedom issue, Khalil's case is weaker than the Nazi's. Khalil would retain his right to espouse antisemitic hate speech even if he were deported. He could do it by Zoom, and his Zoom casts would be heard by his millions of bigoted supporters on Columbia and other campuses. Moreover, Khalid is far from being a poster child for freedom of speech or academic freedom: He and his group have denied these rights to Jewish students and faculty members by preventing them from going to classes, by disrupting classes, and by harassing those with opposing views.

So let civil libertarians treat Khalil the way we treated the Nazis in Skokie: Defend his First Amendment right not to be punished—in this case deported—if what he said and did is protected by the First Amendment and if he did not obtain his visa and green card by fraud. But do not defend him on the merits and demerits of what he said and did. Two things can be true at the same time, especially when it comes to freedom of speech: 1) What he said and did may be constitutionally defensible; 2) at the same time, it may be morally condemnable. That may well be the case with Khalil.

C. Case of Anti-Israel Green Card Holder Seized by ICE Could Be a Close Call for Even the Highest of Courts

The Trump administration has arrested and decided to deport Mahmoud Khalil, a green card holder married to an American citizen who was eight months pregnant at the time. His arrest raises important questions relating to the status of permanent residents who have green cards.

The law explicitly authorizes their deportation on a number of specified grounds, including conviction for crimes of moral turpitude, as well as for somewhat vaguer "national security" grounds.

Hundreds of thousands of students and others have signed petitions claiming that Mr. Khalil's arrest violates his rights of free speech. The evidence, though, seems to suggest that he went beyond merely expressing anti-Israel views. He almost certainly trespassed and may have participated in actions that blocked access of Jewish students to classes. Yet he has not been convicted of any crimes of moral turpitude.

As a matter of pure constitutional law, the president would have the right to deport anyone whose presence in America was not in the national interest, but statutes would seem to limit that broad authority. Ultimately, the courts will have to decide whether the scope of presidential power has been constrained by the enactment of congressional legislation. In the meantime, Mr. Khalil has been whisked off to Louisiana, where he is being detained pending the resolution of the deportation demand.

The reason he was moved a thousand miles away from his home probably has more to do with judge shopping than with safety concerns. He is less likely to find a sympathetic judge in Louisiana than he might be in New York or the District of Columbia. Regardless of where the case is initially brought, it may ultimately end up in the Supreme Court, testing the issue of executive authority. Much will depend on the evidence produced by the government in support of deportation.

Unless the government can prove by a standard lower than proof beyond a reasonable doubt that he meets the criteria for deportation, it may well lose. The decision whether to try him for crimes of moral turpitude also depends on the evidence. It depends, too, on the decisions by New York and federal prosecutors whether to bring the criminal case. Such a case could only be brought in New York where his alleged crimes may have occurred.

So this is not a slam dunk for the government. Nor should it be. A delicate balance must be struck between the free speech rights of even the most obnoxious, anti-American, antisemitic, and anti-free-speech zealots and the rights of those who he may have been victimized by his repressive actions.

The vast majority of Americans would almost certainly want to see Mr. Khalil deported, but when it comes to free speech, the majority does not rule—the First Amendment does. So, depending on the evidence, this may prove to be an important First Amendment case challenging the power of the executive in the context of deportation.

In resolving this conflict, the courts should consider two related First Amendment rights: the right of the non-American citizen to express controversial views and the right of American citizens to hear such views.

It is certainly possible that the need to resolve these conflicting rights may be mooted by the evidence. If the government is able to prove that his actions went beyond First Amendment protected speech, the courts may well resolve the issue in favor of the government. The presumption of innocence operates in criminal cases as a matter of law. It may also have applicability in civil cases as a matter of policy.

In the end, no one should have sympathy for Mr. Khalil as an individual, as an advocate, or as an ideologue. His views, as he himself has expressed them, are despicable, anti-American, antisemitic, and intolerant of others. Yet the First Amendment knows no such things as a false or despicable idea. All ideas are created equal as a matter of constitutional law, though they are far from equal as a matter of morality.

D. Are Trump's Campus Funding Cuts an Attack or Defense of Free Speech?

The Trump administration's decision to cut $400 million of federal grants to Columbia University is intended to influence the actions of university administrators. Its goal is to incentivize them to do more to protect Jewish and pro-Israel students from antisemitic harassment.

Will this curtail peaceful and thus legitimate free speech on affected university campuses? The ACLU says it will deter legitimate protests against Israel. Anti-Israel activists go even further—Peter Beinart warns that "we are witnessing the greatest assault on campus free speech in decades."

What these critics fail to acknowledge is that there are dangers to free speech on both sides—in inaction as well as overreaction.

The cutoff of financial support is aimed at universities that do not do enough to protect the rights of Jewish and Zionist students to attend classes, wear Jewish-identifying symbols such as Stars of David and yarmulkes, and to demonstrate and leaflet in support of Israel without fear of harassment or attack by masked agitators.

There is, of course, always the danger that campus administrators might go too far in protecting Jewish students by limiting peaceful anti-Israel protests. But there is little evidence that the legitimate free-speech rights of anti-Israel peaceful protesters are being abridged. The focus is and should be on unlawful conduct that falls outside the protection of free speech, such as blocking access, interfering with classes, and intimidating students. Universities should not interfere with peaceful and lawful anti-Israel demonstrations.

Columbia is a private institution, not legally bound by the First Amendment, although it claims to adhere to its spirit. It also claims to apply a single content-neutral standard to all freedom of expression. Pursuant to these principles, it should allow peaceful anti-Israel protesters to say anything about Israel, Zionism, and

Jews that it would allow anti-Black, anti-gay, anti-transgender, and anti-abortion demonstrators to say about those groups and issues.

But of course, no university, private or public, would allow racist or sexist demonstrators to call for the lynching of Blacks, the raping of women, or discrimination based on reproductive or identity choices.

The First Amendment does not prohibit private universities from applying a double standard against Jews and Zionists or in favor of groups deemed to be privileged under the affirmative action guidelines of DEI or intersectionality. But the government, in deciding whether to give taxpayer money to private or public institutions, does have the power to withhold funds from schools that apply invidious standards.

No university has the right to receive taxpayer grants. It must show that such grants promote the national interest rather than some partisan ideology. Grants for medical and scientific research promote the national interest. Many other grants do not.

Consider, for example, Barnard's Department of Women's, Gender, and Sexuality Studies, whose website contains an image of a shirt printed with the phrase, "Smash the white supremacis(t) hetero-patriarchy."

I don't know whether federal money goes directly to this and other "studies" or "programs" with comparably ideological and controversial goals, but money is fungible—and therein lies the problem. A $400 million cut from Columbia will affect the entire university, including medical and scientific research. It would be far more effective and selective if funding could be cut back only from programs that do not serve the public interest.

It will not be easy to target with precision the evils that are intended to be addressed by the Trump tactic of cutting funding to universities that do not do enough to protect Jewish and Zionist students. But it is worth trying.

Trump to Harvard

The priority should be to send the message to universities that legitimate, single-standard, peaceful protests against Israel, Zionism, or any other nation or ideology must be permitted in the interests of free speech and academic freedom. An equally important priority is to protect the rights of Jewish and Zionist students and faculty to their free speech, safety, security, and academic freedom.

Striking the appropriate balance is among the most important roles of universities and government-granting agencies. It can be and should be accomplished, despite its challenges.

E. Cut Federal Funding to Barnard

President Donald Trump has pledged to cut federal funding to schools that do not protect Jewish students from antisemitic harassment and violence. The best place to begin this process is Barnard College in New York City. Cutting funding to major research universities threatens cutbacks on grants for medical and other important scientific research. Barnard College, on the other hand, is not a university. It does not have a medical school. Its faculty does little or no research that would affect Americans on a day-to-day basis. Cutting off federal aid to Barnard would have few negative impacts on issues that legitimately concern Americans, especially if it focuses on discriminatory actions and does not interfere with protected free speech.

Barnard has become the poster child for anti-American, antisemitic, and anti-decent activities. Its radical "studies" departments are propaganda mills that teach students what to think rather than how to think. Its mission is described as follows:

> WGSS is dedicated to linking inquiry and action, theory and practice, scholarship and feminism. We work with our colleagues in Africana Studies, American Studies, and the Barnard Center for Research on Women to develop analyses and practices that address the current moment,

> including scholarly discussions, student projects with local communities, videos on transformative justice . . .

In other words, this women's studies department has little to do with scholarship, teaching, or learning. It has everything to do with advocacy. It would never hire an eminent scholar whose research led him or her to question the woke narratives of "smash the white supremacis(t) hetero-patriarchy." That is true of many other specialized studies departments at Barnard.

It is not surprising therefore that Barnard has become the incubator for anti-American, anti-Israel, and antisemitic protests. Signs at these protests call for "war" and "intifada." Nor is the war limited to Israel. It is directed against Americans as well. The protests involve masked students, faculty, and non-students who occupy buildings, prevent Jewish students from attending classes, and threaten to close down the college unless it divests from Israel and takes other bigoted actions.

When two Barnard students were expelled for disturbing a class at Columbia University taught by an Israeli professor, protesters occupied Barnard's Milstein Hall—named after a Jewish donor—and demanded that these expulsions be rescinded. The college administration, instead of disciplining students who break the rules and the law, negotiated with them. Cutting off funding from Barnard will not hurt students who want a real education, because Barnard students can enroll in courses at Columbia, which is affiliated with Barnard. It will put an end to the propaganda "courses," "studies," and "programs" in which Barnard seems to specialize.

It may also eventually cause the closing down of Barnard, because colleges depend on federal funding to supplement tuition and contributions from alumni. Donations from alumni are down recently, for understandable reasons.

Barnard's closure would be no great loss. Qualified students could transfer to Columbia or other universities with no real negative implications. If federal funding is what is keeping Barnard afloat, it deserves to sink.

Higher education needs a shot across the bow, and there is no better target than Barnard. Others may follow if they persist in destroying objective education and substituting ideological propaganda. Taxpayers should not be funding such bigoted enterprises.

It is imperative that freedom of speech, protected by the First Amendment, not be compromised by the government. Barnard is a private institution not bound by that amendment. Moreover, those activities that would cause a shutdown of federal funding are not covered by freedom of speech. They consist largely of physical actions, such as trespassing, blocking access, harassment, and other forms of intimidation. Pure protests consisting of speech should not be a basis for defunding.

Federal funding is not a right. Every institution that seeks taxpayer funding must earn that privilege by what it is contributing to our nation. Barnard no longer deserves our financial or other support. Neither do other colleges and universities that do not protect Jewish students and faculty from harassment and intimidation on campus.

Most university administrators have failed to provide such protection because they are fearful of the reaction from radical students and faculty in their midst. There must be external pressures to incentivize cowardly administrators to do the right thing. Cutting off federal funding from the worst offenders, such as Barnard, would be a good beginning.

F. Harvard Surrenders! University Professor ALAN DERSHOWITZ Reveals the Secret Deal Being Struck with Trump . . . and It'll Make His Woke Colleagues Furious

Many in the mainstream media and academia are cheering on Harvard University as this storied institution has, in the words of the *New York Times*, "decided to fight the Trump administration." But as a Harvard faculty member for more than sixty years, I can tell you that's not quite what is actually happening.

Don't tell Harvard's left-wing professors, but the university seems ready to make a deal with President Trump. The president upped the ante after threatening to withdraw the university's tax-exempt status and gut nearly $2.3 billion in federal funding over a list of grievances, including Harvard's failure to address an explosion of antisemitic hatred in classrooms and on campus.

"Everyone knows that Harvard has 'lost its way,'" Trump posted on Truth Social. "Harvard is a JOKE, teaches Hate and Stupidity, and should no longer receive Federal Funds."

You may have expected Harvard's president, Alan Garber, a man I know and admire, to be defiant in the face of such an onslaught, and while he is putting up a combative front, he seems to be preparing to negotiate a settlement. That's something that legions of far-left academicians and advisers may find abhorrent. But it's the reality.

While Harvard University is older than the US, richer than many countries (with its $50 billion endowment), and among the most influential academic institutions in the world, it depends on federal research grants, tax-deductible contributions from alumni, and tax exemptions on its profits to perform its educational and research functions.

Indeed, Garber has issued a bellicose response to Trump in the form of a letter, publicly refusing to compromise the academic independence of the institution, writing: "No government—regardless of which party is in power—should dictate what private universities can teach, whom they can admit and hire, and which areas of study and inquiry they can pursue."

That is a sentiment that I largely agree with. But at the same time, Harvard has retained lawyers—Ballard Partners—who are close to Trump and his administration and have a history of arranging complex agreements.

Garber's missive is clearly intended to placate Harvard's largely left-wing faculty and administrators, for whom any capitulation to Trump would be academic treason. Defending the independence of the university from any governmental interference, especially from the Trump administration, is required for any university president to survive.

Witness what happened when Columbia University's temporary president, Dr. Katrina Armstrong, appeared to capitulate to White House demands last month and, among other reforms, appoint a new official to oversee departments that offer biased courses on the Middle East. Armstrong was unceremoniously pressured to resign.

For all of Garber's maneuvering, he surely realizes that he is unlikely to emerge victorious from a long, drawn-out courtroom confrontation with Trump. He also must know that the Trump administration would benefit politically from a courtroom fight with Harvard, regardless of the legal outcome that is anything but certain. So, instead, Harvard has sent a more subtle message to the Trump administration by retaining lawyers that he can work with.

Perhaps the Trump administration has been overbroad in demands to "audit" the views of students and staff, exert more influence over course material, and slash funds from legitimate research projects. However, these are complex and nuanced issues, but for many academics, that choice is simple: Whatever side Trump is on is wrong.

Well, reforming our corrupted academic elitist class and fighting antisemitic bigotry is not wrong. That is why I support a negotiated compromise. In fact, it is essential. The truth is that many of the government's demands are quite reasonable and necessary.

Harvard does have a serious lack of intellectual, ideological, and political diversity. It is largely a left-wing institution where many points of view are effectively muzzled, largely by self-censorship and peer pressure.

To give one very personal illustration: For fifty years, I was among the most popular faculty members, teaching and lecturing to over 10,000 students. But since October 7, 2023, when Hamas perpetrated the deadliest attack on Jews since the Holocaust, I have never once been invited to present my centrist pro-Israel position on campus. Even before that, the one time I was invited by a student group, my talk had to be moved off campus for fear of my safety.

Dozens of students have communicated with me in recent years about how they feel silenced. These include not only Jewish and Zionist students but also Christian and conservative students. The same is true for some faculty members.

Harvard's culture is infected by a deeply rooted cultural bias that even President Trump cannot quickly cure. This is largely attributable to Harvard's tenured faculty, whose rehabilitation is nearly impossible and utterly impractical, because these professors—whose jobs are contractually protected—are essentially accountable to no one. That academic freedom, while justified in many ways, has been abused for decades.

The oppressive campus culture is also due to "programs" and departments that are inherently ideological. These include Women Studies, Gay Studies, Black Studies, and yes, Jewish Studies departments. These divisions and similar ones tend to be more ideological than academic. In addition, there are the racial, ethnic, and gender offices, such as diversity, equity, and inclusion (DEI). These entrenched bureaucracies have undue influence.

Harvard has already settled two lawsuits brought by several Jewish students and organizations alleging antisemitism on campus, and—without admitting any wrongdoing—the university has pledged to do more to confront the biases that result in de facto discrimination against certain students and faculty. A negotiated settlement between Harvard and the Trump administration may be another step toward reform, but it cannot be the last.

Finally, for those who claim that their defense of university autonomy and academic freedom is ideologically neutral, it is important to remember the 1950s, when I was a college student. In those bad old days, many recalcitrant southern universities had been forced by the federal government to integrate their student bodies, yet the schools were still tolerating the harassment of African American students and teaching racist curricula.

Had the federal government threatened to withhold funding from such racist universities unless there were changes, many liberals, civil libertarians, and advocates of academic freedom would have applauded.

Now that the shoe is on the other foot, many progressive academics are taking exactly the opposite position they would've taken back in the 1950s.

For them, it's about politics, not principles.

For me, it's about principles, consistency, and neutrality.

G. Need to Disable Iran's Nuclear Weapons Program More Compelling than Ever

Israel's degradation of Iranian surrogates, especially Hamas and Hezbollah, makes the need to disable Iran's nuclear weapons program more compelling than ever before.

Iran's only remaining weapon in its long-declared goal of destroying the nation-state of the Jewish people is the nuclear arsenal it is building. It is more likely now that if Iran could build a small nuclear arsenal with a working delivery system, it would use it either as a credible deterrent threat against Israel or as a weapon of mass destruction. Nothing is more dangerous than a nuclear power that lacks conventional weapons.

Iran does not have a viable army, air force, or navy. In a direct military confrontation with Israel, it would lose badly and quickly, regardless of whether the United States assisted Israel. That is why Iran has not attacked Israel after the Israel Defense Forces' destruction of its air defenses in 2024. It does not want to give Israel a justification for further military action, but the mullahs have not given up on their religious dream to end the "Zionist entity" and "the small Satan."

They and their military and intelligence wings still believe, as Akbar Hashemi Rafsanjani, the former president of Iran, once put it, that Israel is "a one-bomb state" whose existence would be terminated by a single successful nuclear bomb attack. A United Nations report says Iran has enough weapons-grade uranium to produce six nuclear weapons. No Israeli defense system, no matter how sophisticated, could guarantee that a single rocket with a nuclear warhead could not make it through Israel's amazing domes, slings, and other high-tech defenses.

Regardless of the likelihood of such a military nightmare becoming a reality, Israel could never take that risk, especially after its disastrous intelligence failure of October 7, 2023. Underreaction almost always causes overreaction, and Israel will not risk another more serious underreaction to a nuclear threat from Iran.

President Trump strongly believes that he can prevent a nuclear-armed Iran by diplomatic rather than military means. He believes that a stronger, longer-lasting agreement would be sufficient to prevent Iran from developing a nuclear arsenal. He has nominated Elbridge Colby to be the undersecretary of defense for policy.

Mr. Colby has said that "Washington, Tel Aviv, and their associates can deter Iran from transgressing their vital interest even if Tehran gets a nuclear weapon." It is doubtful that Israeli prime minister Benjamin Netanyahu agrees with that view. What we don't know is whether the Trump administration would try to persuade Israel to forgo or postpone military action in deference to Mr. Trump's desire to settle the matter through a deal or deterrence.

One possibility that combines Mr. Trump's preference for a tough deal with Israel's need to be certain that Iran gets no closer to a deliverable nuclear bomb is for Mr. Trump to offer a deal with an ultimatum. The ultimatum would be for Iran to agree to begin to dismantle its nuclear weapons program immediately, with a deadline for completion within several months. Failure to comply with that deadline completely transparently would result in a joint military action to achieve that result or, at the very least, a green light to Israel to finish the job.

The only permanent road to enduring peace throughout the Middle East would require regime change and the democratization of Iran. In the absence of an internal revolution, this would require external force, which the Trump administration seems not to support. Arab nations and Israel would welcome regime change, but it seems unlikely even in the face of strong opposition to the mullahs from the Iranian street.

Hardly anyone in the region wants to see a nuclear-armed Iran. Neither do the United States or Europe. The question is how to stop it. The status quo under which Iran will almost certainly move toward a nuclear arsenal—how quickly is uncertain—is unacceptable, especially to Israel. At the moment, Messrs. Trump and Netanyahu have no direct conflict. Both have pledged that Iran will never be allowed to develop a nuclear weapon. However, they may soon disagree on the means necessary to achieve that mutually desired goal and timing.

It is unlikely that they will end up in the kind of open conflict we saw in the Oval Office between Mr. Trump and Ukrainian president Volodymyr Zelenskyy, but it is certainly possible that the

Trump administration will try to stop Israel from attacking Iran's nuclear sites on its preferred schedule. That would be a shame, because a military attack shortly may be the surest way of bringing about enduring peace throughout the increasingly volatile and dangerous Middle East.

H. Was the *Atlantic*'s Goldberg Wrong in Not Immediately Leaving the Chat?

An important question of journalistic ethics has been largely ignored in the discussion about the inclusion of the *Atlantic* editor-in-chief in a secret government chat.

Obviously, the primary responsibility for adding Jeffrey Goldberg to the Signal chat was with the government official who negligently included him. But as soon as Goldberg realized he had been inadvertently and improperly included in the chat, should he have immediately notified the government officials to be removed? Would he have acted differently if he had been inadvertently included in a chat by officials of the prior administration, which he supported, rather than this administration which he opposes?

I have experienced similar situations on several occasions. As a lawyer, I have sometimes been inadvertently included on an email thread that was intended only for the other side of a case. As soon as I saw my name on the list and realized that it was inadvertent, I notified the other side and destroyed any and all communications from that group, without reading them. That was the ethical thing to do, even though my own client would have secured a tactical advantage if I had remained on the thread and learned the other side's secrets.

As Secretary of State Henry Stimson once put it, "Gentlemen do not read other gentlemen's mail." That may overstate it in the context of intelligence gathering, but it is generally a good rule to live by in many other contexts.

Similarly, Goldberg gained an enormous reportorial and

Trump to Harvard

personal advantage from remaining in the chat without disclosing his presence. But should he have done so? Or was he ethically bound to disclose what had to be obvious to him: His inclusion was inadvertent and reflected a dangerous threat to national security?

Journalists often feel that they have only one responsibility, and that they can employ any means to justify the noble end of promoting that responsibility: obtaining all possible information, regardless of its cost to others.

Goldberg did nothing illegal by remaining in the chat, nor did he violate loosely defined journalistic ethics (an oxymoron to many!). But I believe he did the wrong thing. Goldberg should have immediately notified the proper authorities that they had endangered national security by including him in the chat. Had he done so, he would have had a far less interesting story to report, but he would have served the national interest.

This is not the first time journalists have been confronted with a conflict between their journalistic obligation to get the story and their patriotic obligation not to endanger national security. History is filled with situations where journalists could have disclosed dangerous information but declined to do so.

To be sure, Goldberg did not disclose the sensitive information. He kept it to himself and presumably his colleagues. He was not responsible for affirmatively making a dangerous disclosure. He simply failed to alert the authorities to their mistake at the earliest possible time, and by doing so reaped a journalistic advantage. So the question is a nuanced one, without a simple answer.

We as a nation were fortunate that no harm came from the erroneous inclusion of Goldberg on the chat. Indeed, in retrospect, some benefit may have occurred, because nothing like this will ever happen again. As a result of the disclosure of this embarrassing mistake, the Trump administration will double down on its efforts to prevent any future unauthorized disclosure of secret information.

What will likely recur, however, is the ethical question posed by being inadvertently included in secret communications.

This issue should be debated both in the journalistic community and in Congress. There ought to be some ethical guidelines as to how a responsible journalist should handle the situation in which Goldberg found himself. There can also be a legal response. Congress could enact a law compelling anyone who inadvertently receives what was obviously not intended for his eyes and ears. Such a law would obviate the ethical issue by compelling journalists to disclose their inadvertent inclusion in a secret chat.

One thing is clear: The decision whether to remain surreptitiously on what is obviously a secret chat is an issue worthy of discussion. It is too important to leave to the unguided discretion of a journalist who may not be unbiased.

I. Gaza: There Are Precedents for Moving People to Secure Peace

The immediate reaction by pundits to President Trump's out-of-the-box proposals regarding the Gaza Strip has been knee-jerk rejection. Few, however, have proposed better alternatives. Certainly, a return to the status quo would be untenable. It would result in more terrorism, more destruction, more deaths, and less peace. We need the kind of new thinking that occurred after the defeat of Nazi Germany and Japan at the end of World War II.

We can learn from history that the relocation of people is sometimes necessary to secure an enduring peace. Ethnic Germans had lived in Sudetenland for generations. Their presence there had played a significant role in the Nazi aggression against Czechoslovakia that led to World War II. After the defeat of Germany, millions of ethnic Germans were relocated out of Sudetenland. This helped bring about enduring peace in Central Europe.

Similarly, the relocation of many Indian and Pakistani residents after the end of British colonial rule helped stabilize that area.

Wars result in population movements, especially for residents of nations that initiated the wars. Consider the German city of Konigsberg, which had been an important part of Germany for centuries. When the Soviet Union defeated Germany, it transferred nearly the entire German population of Konigsberg, renamed it Kaliningrad, repopulated it with ethnic Russians, and annexed it to the Soviet Union, which was hundreds of miles away.

World leaders, including Winston Churchill and President Franklin Delano Roosevelt, deemed these population transfers necessary. They were not without serious difficulties, including the deaths of some innocent people, but history has demonstrated that they were worth the cost.

Peace is more important than place, and if an enduring peace in the Middle East could be achieved with temporary or even longer-term population transfers, it may be worth considering. Deploying loaded terms such as "ethnic cleansing" and "population transfers" does not solve what has long appeared to be the intractable problems associated with the Gaza Strip, which was originally part of Egypt, then occupied by Israel, then returned to Palestinian control, and ultimately taken over in a coup by the terrorists of Hamas.

Mr. Trump's initial proposal is not written in stone. Like other Trump initiatives, it is provocative and designed to shake up the status quo. There are many possible variations, including temporary US control over what Mr. Trump correctly describes as demolition sites. The United States, with the assistance of Arab and Muslim nations, could take over portions of the Gaza Strip, destroy the terrorist tunnels underneath the land, and rebuild it in a way that minimizes the prospects of remilitarization by Hamas. Palestinian families could then be returned to the rebuilt areas after being vetted to exclude Hamas terrorists and supporters. This will not be easy, but neither would any other solution to the Gaza problem.

The ultimate goal of a completely rebuilt, demilitarized "Singapore on the Mediterranean" will not be easy to achieve. But it may be worth trying.

To begin with, Palestinian residents of areas subject to reconstruction could be generously compensated for their dislocation by funds provided by wealthy Arab states in the region. It is inevitable, however, that some Palestinian residents of Gaza will refuse to move, even temporarily, for fear that they will never be allowed to return. It is also likely that Hamas would threaten any residents who accepted payment to move. Accordingly, some degree of compulsion would be necessary as it was in Sudetenland, India, Pakistan, and Konigsberg. When it comes to peace in Gaza, there are no free lunches—only the comparative costs of imperfect actions versus disastrous nonactions.

A demilitarized Gaza would dramatically increase the chances of a broader resolution to the Israel-Palestinian conflict. It would open the door to new ideas about the governance of the West Bank. It might encourage the Arab states, especially Saudi Arabia, to join the Abraham Accords. A return to the status quo, with Gaza remaining under the control of terrorist groups and rebuilding its tunnels, holds no similar prospects for an enduring peace.

So, let thoughtful people with goodwill think hard about alternatives to a return to the status quo. There will be no perfect solution. Every plan will have its pitfall, every idea its detractors, and every alternative its downside. But let's give credit where credit is due: Mr. Trump has introduced the first new idea in the many years in which old ideas have failed.

J. Why Have So Many Israelis and Jews Moved to the Right?

There can be little doubt that over the last quarter of a century,

Israeli voters have moved from the left to the center, and now to the right. The same is true, though to a somewhat lesser degree, of Israeli supporters in the United States, Great Britain, Canada, and other countries with significant Jewish populations. The primary reason is obvious: The left has turned against Israel and against its supporters.

Jews have traditionally been on the left side of politics both in Israel and in the diaspora. When Israel was first established, it had widespread support among the left, even among the extreme left. At its founding, Israel was a socialist democracy surrounded by reactionary Arab dictatorships. Not surprisingly, the Soviet Union supported its establishment in 1948, and Czechoslovakia even supplied it with arms to defend itself against invading Arab nations. This all changed in the 1960s when the Soviet Union decided to abandon left-wing Israel and support the right-wing Arab states that were seeking Israel's destruction. The reason for this switch was purely power politics: The undemocratic Arab states were rich in natural resources, especially oil and gas; they also had geographical advantages such as the Suez Canal. Israel on the other hand was an agrarian socialist state with few natural or geographic resources; they exported Jaffa oranges and mud from the Dead Sea.

When the Soviet Union turned against Israel and in favor of Arab tyrannies, the European and American hard-left fell in line. Euro-communist parties followed the lead of the Soviet Union, as did the American Communist party. Most moderate leftists continued to support Israel, especially during the Six Day War in 1967.

Israeli voters generally continued to support left-wing candidates until 1977, when Menachem Begin won a surprising victory. Since that time, the trend among Israeli voters has been slightly right, though left-wing candidates, such as Yitzhak Rabin and Ehud Barak won elections in 1974, 1992, and 1999.

Then, two developments began to move Israeli voters

discernibly to the right. The first was the immigration of hundreds of thousands of Soviet Jews into Israel. These Jews had experienced discrimination and persecution from Communist regimes throughout the Soviet Union. Not surprisingly, they did not trust the left. These new immigrants asserted themselves politically and formed alliances primarily with center-right and right-wing parties.

Israel is a vibrant and dynamic democracy, where outcomes depend on the experiences, history, and ideology of the voters. So the influx of anti-Communist Soviet Jews had an immediate impact on Israeli politics, moving it to the right.

The second reason for the rightward movement by Israeli voters is the Arab rejectionism of Israeli peace offers. The most striking example of this phenomenon was the 2000–2001 peace initiative by liberal prime minister Ehud Barak and American president Bill Clinton.

Here is the way Clinton characterized the offer:

[The] peace deal that we had worked out . . . would have given the Palestinians a state in 96% of the West Bank and 4% of Israel, and they got to choose where the 4% of Israel was. So they would have the effect of the same land of all the West Bank. They would have a capital in east Jerusalem. . . . All this was offered including . . . a capital in east Jerusalem and two of the four quadrants of the old city of Jerusalem confirmed by the Israeli Prime Minister Ehud Barack and his cabinet, and they said no, and I think part of it is that Hamas did not care about a homeland for the Palestinians. They wanted to kill Israelis and make Israel uninhabitable.

This rejection of a two-state solution was accompanied by an intifada in which thousands of Israeli and Palestinian civilians were killed. This led to the weakening of the Israeli left and the strengthening of the right. Many centrist Israeli voters grew frustrated with the failed efforts of the "peace camp" to achieve a two-state solution through negotiation and compromise. Israelis began to believe that terrorism could be prevented and/or deterred only through military actions.

Then came Hamas. In 2005, Israel's conservative prime minister Ariel Sharon unilaterally ended Israel's occupation of Gaza and turned Israeli equipment over to Palestinian leaders in an effort to create a viable Palestinian enclave—Singapore on the Mediterranean. Hamas then proceeded to murder Palestinian authority leaders and take over the Gaza Strip in an unlawful coup. Hamas then fired rockets into Israel for years. This belligerency culminated in the October 7 massacres and kidnappings. The victims were primarily Israeli leftists and peaceniks who are active in efforts to bring about a two-state solution. Not surprisingly, October 7 weakened the left and strengthened the right.

The reaction of the left to October 7, and the positive support given by many to the Hamas barbarism, moved many Jews out of their traditional left-wing base and toward a more conservative perspective.

The above analysis is not intended either to justify or criticize this obvious rightward movement among many Israelis and their supporters around the world. It is intended to explain a phenomenon that many seem not to understand. It should be expected that when the left turns against a nation and its supporters and the right turns toward them, there will be a change in attitudes and voting patterns. Many people somehow believe, however, that Israelis and Jews should be different: They should continue to support the left even though the left has abandoned them. But to expect Israelis and Jews to act against their interest is to impose an unacceptable double standard.

K. Today's Most Pressing Human Rights Violation: Malignant Antisemitism

I have spent my life defending the human and civil rights of African Americans, women, gays, and other discriminated-against groups. Though discrimination against these groups persists, it is far less than in past, and the trajectory is in their favor. Not so for Jews and Israelis. Antisemitism, often disguised as anti-Zionism, is on the rise and the trajectory is deeply discouraging, because the anti-Jewish bigotry—unlike other bigotries—is most prevalent among the young and better educated, who will determine our future. All the polls show that that the greatest increase in hatred is against Jews and their state.

Accordingly, the problem of antisemitism must be placed high on the agenda of anyone who claims to be a supporter of human rights and civil liberties. Yet traditional groups that purport to support these rights have not only ignored the attack on Jews, many of them have actively supported the organizations and individuals who have promoted antisemitism and anti-Zionism. I'm not talking about defending the constitutional rights of those with whom you disagree. That is commendable. I'm talking about making heroes of bigots who single out Jews for condemnation, harassment, and violation of their human rights. It is as if Jews are either not "human" or their "rights" are not important. That is the message of "intersectionality," which divides the world into oppressed and oppressors, with the Jews as oppressors and deniers of basic right to the oppressed.

This is ironic because Jews have been instrumental in developing and implementing civil liberties and human rights. The very concept of human rights was developed by the Jewish Holocaust survivor who drafted the Universal Declaration of Human Rights. Jews were instrumental in the civil rights movement in the South during the 1960s (I know because I was there). Jews have been at the forefront of the civil liberties movement, with many—including me—on the national board of the ACLU. Now these concepts have been turned on their head and directed against Jews and their nation-state, despite the fact that Jews are still among the most liberal elements among every nation, and that Israel, despite its turn to the right, is the most liberal nation in the Middle East and one of the most civil libertarian in the world.

The major weapon currently directed at Jews and their state is the double standard: Attacks, verbal and physical, that would never be tolerated against Blacks, gays, and other minorities are not only tolerated, but often justified when directed at Jews. The examples of this double standard are too many to catalogue, but they include differential treatment of antisemitic speech on campuses, widespread support of Hamas, an organization that is openly homophobic, sexist, racist, and antisemitic. Even those who argue that what we are experiencing is anti-Zionism not antisemitism, and that the former is entirely legitimate, must acknowledge the double standard against Israel as compared with far worse violators. An invidious double standard is itself bigotry, and when directed against Jews and their state, it is the oldest and most enduring form of bigotry.

So this is a call to all those—young and old—who regard themselves as advocates of human and civil rights and liberties. Prioritize the rights of those who are the most discriminated against today, and are likely to be even more discriminated against tomorrow and in years to come. Jews and Zionists are the only groups against whom discrimination and the application of a double standard is legitimized by so many in academia, the media, and the political left. They are the only groups against whom discrimination is trending and increasing. Only you—especially non-Jews—can reverse this dangerous and immoral trend. And you can do it in the ways we reversed earlier trends against the rights of Blacks, women, gays, and other discriminated-against groups. The first step is to recognize and acknowledge that the double standard currently being applied against the Jews and their state is a denial of their most basic rights and liberties. Then good people of every background must unite to protect the rights of Jews with the same vigor that Jews have shown in defending the rights of others.

In the 1930s, too many people—including faculty and students at elite universities—stood on the wrong side of history, either by their complicity or silence. This is the time to get on the right side of decency by prioritizing the human and civil rights of the group currently most at risk of losing these rights, namely, Jews.

L. Israel's Preemptive Attack Is Legally, Morally, and Diplomatically Justified

In my just-published book, *The Preventive State*, I make the following case for a preemptive military strike against Iran's nascent nuclear arsenal:

> If [diplomacy] fails and if it becomes likely that Iran is about to cross the threshold into making a deliverable nuclear weapon, the pressure on Israel to act, with or without the assistance and/or approval of the United States, will increase considerably. . . .
>
> No democracy can afford to wait until such a threat against its civilian population is imminent. Israel and the United States should have the right under international law to protect their civilians and soldiers from a threatened nuclear holocaust, and that right must include—if that is the only realistic option—preemptive military action of the sort taken by Israel against the Iraqi nuclear

reactor at Osirak in 1981, especially if such action can again be taken without an unreasonable number of civilian casualties.

International law authorizes preemptive military action when reasonably necessary to prevent nuclear attacks on civilian populations. Even if the number of likely casualties on both sides is high in the current war between Israel and Iran, there may be a cost-benefit case for preventive military action, because the cost of not taking such action may be far greater.

In some respects, Israel's recent attack can be justified as reactive rather than preemptive or preventive. It was a legitimate response to Iran's direct missile attacks during this past year, as well as its indirect attacks through its surrogates in Yemen, Lebanon, and Gaza. In any event, preemptive action was necessary.

A prime example of the cost of the false negative of not taking preventive military action is provided by not-so-distant history. In the mid-1930s, after Hitler came to power and began building a military machine in violation of the Versailles Treaty, Britain and France—which were strong militarily but war-weary—could have taken preventive military action against a still weak, but war hungry, Germany. Joseph Goebbels was surprised that "they didn't do it"—until it was too late. Tens of millions of innocent people died as a result of this false negative failure to act.

Had Israel failed to act against Iran by last week, such a "false negative" could have resulted in millions of deaths from a nuclear armed fanatical regime that has pledged to destroy "the Zionist devil." We will never know for certain what harms Israel's preemptive action may have prevented, because history is blind to the predictive future. Had Great Britain and France decided to take preventive military action in the mid-1930s, and done so successfully, no one would ever know *what* was prevented. If a leader, say

Churchill, had been in a position to act on his fear that Hitler would kill tens of millions of people unless he was stopped at <u>that</u> time by preventive military action, the leader would have been disbelieved, even mocked, as George W. Bush was for taking military action against Iraq's suspected nuclear arsenal in 2003. Had Great Britain and France engaged in preventive military action in the 1930s that resulted in, say, the deaths of ten thousand German and five thousand British and French soldiers and civilians, the leaders who undertook such a military adventure would been condemned as warmongers, because no one would ever know how many deaths they prevented by the sacrifice of those fifteen thousand lives. Ignorance of the hypothetical future is often the reason for failure to act in the present. Had Great Britian and France acted, everyone would know about the fifteen thousand deaths their action caused, while no one would know about the tens of millions of lives their action saved.

We know about the tens of millions of deaths these leaders indirectly caused—or at least made possible—by not taking preventive military action, but we don't accuse them of actually causing these deaths, because inaction that indirectly leads to death is not generally blamed as much as action that directly and visibly produces a body count. That is the dilemma of invisible false negatives in failing to take preventive military action.

A preventive attack would not have been cost free, and it was not undertaken because the British and French did not accurately predict and assess the cost of not acting. The result was a catastrophic false negative.

Benjamin Netanyahu has been faulted—largely by left-wing Democrats and radicals—on the ground that he acted too quickly, failing to wait for the outcome of talks that might have resulted in a diplomatic resolution. But a satisfactory deal that would have absolutely assured that Iran would never obtain nuclear weapons was never likely, because Iran insisted on its "right" to enrich, and enrichment is a path to weaponization.

It seems clear that Iran was using the negotiations to buy time to move toward a nuclear arsenal. Its goal was to get close enough to weaponization so as to make it too risky to attack its radioactive facilities.

So Netanyahu was right, as a matter of law, morality, and diplomacy, to do <u>what</u> he did <u>when</u> he did it.

Conclusion

The combination of factors described above—lower admission requirements, higher (or no) grades for lower quality work, substitution of ideological advocacy for objective scholarship, governance structures, and criteria that encourage these aberrations from academic standards—has changed Harvard and other universities from meritocracy to mediocracy in one generation. This reduction in quality has affected not only the student body but the faculty as well. In order to cover up this obvious diminution in academic and scholarly standards, the faculty and administration have taken steps to hide the truth. The end of objective grading and neutral evaluation is among these deceptive tactics. Veritas, the age-old symbol of Harvard, has become mediocris and indignus in a short span of time. This negative trend must be reversed if universities are to return to their Socratic mission of teaching, learning, and increasing truthful knowledge. Compromise is essential to reversing this negative trajectory. It is the goal of this book to offer guidance to negotiating resolutions. This is an ongoing process that seems to be beginning. Let us hope it continues in the best interests of our nation and its educational enterprise.